*out of gratitude*

*Wilhelm Velten and his wife*

„The most important role Dionne has

and encouragement to finish

you are not achieving your goal,

... you will succeed."

played is her continued support

what you start even if it appears

you must persist and ...

Delia Warrick

# My Point

# Of View

## Dionne Warwick

*Index*

# First Preface

There are moments in life, which - for whatever reasons - we would prefer to forget. The kinds of moments where we utter desperate such as "if only I'd known" or "why didn't I see that".

A few months ago I narrowly escaped just such a moment. We were having an internal company discussion about a new autobiography and the person who would deserve to receive the gift of a "written monument" in the years 2003 and 2004. A lot of names were mentioned but none of these promising ideas were followed up.

That evening I watched the presentation of the 2002 Bavarian Film Awards, more for a spot of relaxation than out of a genuine interest in who would receive the most prestigious film award in Germany. The musical item of the evening was performed by Dionne Warwick. At the very same moment that Warwick's performance was announced, the penny dropped: she would of course - Dionne Warwick would deserve to receive her own publication.

But this was not the only coincidence. I also knew that my colleague Giorgio Paolo was a great admirer of this wonderful singer.

I had always had a very high opinion of Dionne myself. During the past decade, no other female singer - in my personal opinion - had been such a successful chart act as she had been. Whether "Don't Make Me Over", "Walk On By" or "That's What Friends Are For": everything Warwick had done in the past forty years turned to gold. But this success was not simply the result of a lot of lucky coincidences. It was based on hard work, discipline and her personal convictions: "If you can think it you can do it !" Even now, Dionne Warwick continues to work on her image, so that the audience get what it expects of her.

## Don´t Make Me Over

After a short meeting in New York City, we suggested that she write a book with us. We agreed fairly quickly on the style and content of the book as well a time at which it should be published. The work itself - meaning the process of creating the book - was always very enjoyable and of a constructive nature, which I have rarely known.

"My Point Of View" is not a novel that provides hours of reading pleasure. But nor is it a book about a world-famous performer which simply lists facts and figures about her career. "My Point Of View" is a book with an almost educational character. The baton is smoothly passed between discussion-provoking ideas, long years of life experience and her own tender views of life - yet without becoming overbearing for the reader.

Mastropaolo & Koblischek Editor hope that "My Point Of View" will give an insight into Warwick's life but also that this book will be an incentive to young people who have chosen the profession of "musician" (as Dionne did early in her life) to recognise the difficulties of the job early on. "My Point Of View" is extremely helpful in this process of self-discovery.

At this point I would like to thank the many people without whom this publication would never have been possible. In particular I would like to thank my late mother, Maria Koblischek, who was always concerned with the production of this book.

I would like to thank Dionne Warwick herself, who made herself available for the many interviews with so much patience and understanding, even when she was very busy with her concerts; Carlos Keyes, one of Warwick's agents, who conducted the initial discussions about this project with pleasure and personal conviction; finally to all who had faith in the creation of the book and supported us in every way.

**I Love Honesty !**

Sven Johann Koblischek
Publishing Director

# Second Preface

*The only connection I have with the wonderful singer Dionne Warwick goes back to a few moments in my youth.*

*It was in the mid-eighties when I had to get up very early to go to school. But before setting off on the trail to school, I would often turn on the television for a bit of background noise. Although in theory I usually turned on the early morning children's programmes, I actually switched on to watch something else.*

*Before the children's programmes started, there were music videos. These music videos were always repeated from the previous day and filled the broadcaster's graveyard slot from midnight to the early hours of the morning. One of these music videos was a particular favourite of mine. It was the song called "That's What Friends Are For". At first I only heard snippets of the song because I switched on the TV too late. Another consequence of this was that I missed the names of both the song and the singer who I felt understood me because of the wonderful lyrics. And yet, even though I only heard a fragment of this beautiful song and had no idea who the artist was, the voice still inspired me so much that I had to hear it every day.*

*Half a year later I had a "déjà vu". At that time I had a crush, not only on that certain "unknown woman", but suddenly also on another woman called Whitney Houston, who it turned out was related to my beloved singer of "That's What Friends Are For". And so it was that through my interest in Whitney, I found out that the singer of my favourite "morning song" was none other than the music legend Dionne Warwick. From that moment on I was obsessed with this fascinating creature.*

**Be Always Open**

*Several years later. I had not heard anything of Dionne Warwick for quite some time. The same applied to her records which I could no longer buy in Germany.*

*One day - at this time I was still a model - I walked out onto the catwalk at a fashion show to the song "Night And Day". The voice coming across the speakers almost made me forgot everything and I felt a wonderful wave of happi - ness. But somehow I couldn't place that voice. Then I discovered that this song was sung by Dionne Warwick. Dionne was once again present in my life and the way she had re-entered it gave me great pleasure and happiness. Later, when the "Friends Can Be Lovers" CD was released, it was a "must" of my CD player. I was (and still am) so obsessed with this fascinating singer Warwick that anyone who visited me had to listen to this record whether they wanted to or not.*

*To my delight, about ten years ago Warwick came to my home town of Hamburg. I was electrified and bought two tickets as soon as the concert was announced. Unfortunately, the concert was postboned for six months but, personally, that did not bother me at all. Quite the reverse, in fact: I was even happier than the first time because, thanks to the delay, I could look forward to Dionne's performance once again. When the time finally arrived, the spell was upon me. After so many years I was finally going see this (and my !) star live. I remember that there was a band, in fact an orchestra, and that Dionne was wearing a stunning trouser suit that evening. I had never seen a powerful stage presence as Warwick before in my life. I was so entranced that I could hardly move. To close the evening she then sang my favourite song "That's What Friends Are For". After the concert, I somehow had a feeling that our paths would maybe cross again.*

*It became reality. The rest is history. But I would like to add that wor- king together on this has been very harmonious and characterised by a great warmth and intimacy between Dionne Warwick and us, the Editor. Let Dionne's wisdom and philosophy spirit you away to discover a new world.*

## Take Care About Your Image

*Giorgio Paolo Mastropaolo - Marketing Director*

# Eternal

# Youth

*or the marvelous*

*behaviour of*

*our children*

„*I mean that Dionne is one of the great voices in popular music.*"

*Todd Hunter*

*The Look Of Love*

*From time to time, people ask me not only how I managed to remain successful in show business for more than forty years, but also how I managed to retain my figure and good looks.*

*To be honest, I have but one answer for this sort of question: "Beauty from within is beauty from without !" If our bodies are governed and guided by harmony, balance and inner peace, this will be reflected in our outward appearance. This view of life sounds very simplistic, but in my opinion it is the best way to keep your body healthy and in good shape for many years.*

*Words like "beauty secret" mean nothing to me. I never knew any beauty secrets and I would consider it rather exhausting and unpleasant to have any. In my opinion, the only people who have beauty secrets are those who believe beauty can or must be kept "secret".*

*And even if beauty really is some kind of secret, the meaning of the word "secret" has long since been stretched to ridiculous lengths by virtue of the fact that the advertising industry not only offers an infinite diversity of beauty secrets in all the media, but also explains them to the general public.*

*„My mother's love for me is unconditional. She taught me everything about life and being a good human being. "*

*David Elliott*

## Here I Am

## Stronger Than Before

„*I love being around Dionne*

*because the atmosphere is*

*love, peace and joy.*"


*David Krause*

Making a large audience privy to beauty secrets seems illogical to me, because it contradicts the meaning of a secret, which is something that should be kept and protected rather than passed on to others.

I also observe that nowadays many people have their own dietary plans, which they follow blindly and with a will of steel, in order to conform to a certain appearance that happens to be en vogue at a given time. Personally, I'm not cut out for that way of thinking.

What has kept me young over the years has been my "inner child" and my love of childlike behaviour. The term "inner child" comes from the realm of psychology and is taken to mean that our inner drives are like children, always wanting to be satisfied.

That's why I love the idea that all human beings (symbolically speaking) have a little child who sits at the edge of their heart, or somewhere in their soul.

## Make It Easy On Yourself

This child must always be cared for and protected, which is what I would call "self protection". I myself protect my "inner child" whenever I can, because it is in my view a reflection of the family I came from. To me it reveals all its strengths and weaknesses, which were passed on to me by my family, and which I have had to come to terms with over the course of my life.

**Age Of Miracles**

My "inner child" is quick to come to the forefront, and that makes her easy to recognise, even after just a brief personal encounter with others. What the inner child enjoys most, though, is to approach life in a playful and amusing manner.

23

## Whisper In The Dark

*Personally, I love the way children behave, and we should – in our own interests – become more conscious of childlike behaviour in our own lives.*

*For as long as I can I remember, I have always kept a little piece of my childhood, of being a child, inside me. I see everything in my life, everything around me, primarily through the eyes of little Dionne, not through the eyes of grown-up Dionne, and I try to make the best of everything I encounter in everyday life.*

*I think that is exactly what we see when we observe children. They are the ones who have a head start over us grown-ups, because their imaginations are unlimited and their ways of thinking are full of fantasy.*

*Like a child, I too sometimes turn something terrible into something beautiful, just as I enjoy — and this is also childlike — having a hearty laugh as often as possible every day. Babies and children are the most important example for us in this case.*

*Isn't the most beautiful sound in the whole world the sound of a baby or a child laughing ?*

*In my opinion, laughter is one of the most important emotions human beings have, the "best medicine" for staying young and lively. But if a person approaches life by treating himself or other people with nothing but grief and disapproval, that person is usually not only a poor worker, but will also soon find himself greeting a frowned and wrinkled face in the mirror.*

*I would never want to go through life with a grumpy attitude, because I want my skin to stay free of wrinkles. I think many people will understand this attitude toward life.*

## Night And Day

Yes, I believe we should all learn a few things from the behaviour of children. It may sound unbelievable at first, but I am positively convinced that when an adult embraces childlike behaviour, it the best proof that he is able to love life on the one hand, and on the other hand, that no matter what may happen to him in the course of his life, he will be capable of taking a position that is both adult and playful, without regrets.

No matter whether events are pleasant or unpleasant: like children, people like those I have just described easily master the tasks life presents to them, because they take the bull by the horns, without too much hesitation or deliberation.

## All Of You

## Remember Your Heart

*With their playful personalities and aided by their life experience, they are able to solve any problems that may arise better and faster. A kind of "eternal childhood" should always be maintained, because it, in my opinion, helps people achieve a more open attitude toward life, as well as more open-mindedness (even in old age). And that will have positive results, because an open-minded personality is always an indication that a person is willing to continue growing and developing within his or her personality.*

*To this day, my life has been entirely shaped by open-mindedness. I have never regretted this attitude toward life. On the contrary, it keeps me young too ! I'm always open to new things that come into my life.*

Of course it's important to be careful, because not every-thing that life has to offer you is the best and most use-ful thing for you. Because of my curiosity I examine everything that comes my way, no matter whether it's personal or professional.

———— ⚜ ————

Not until I have considered it do I decide whom or what I will allow to enter my life. Over the course of my life I have also learned that decisions, thoughts or new tasks are best dealt with if we always nurture the inner-child. I would be delighted if this chapter would give readers some food for thought.

## Anything Goes

„I met Dionne for the first time briefly in Los Angeles

while I was auditioning for the keyboard chair.

She was very gracious and took the time to come

over to me to introduce herself.

The second time we met was just before

our first performance together in the spring of 2003.

She approached me and said : '

Hi, I'm Dionne, welcome to the family !'

and then we walked over to the stage and did the show."

Todd Hunter

Passion

For

Learning

*or the*

*opportunities of*

*a good education*

*Children of the Favela Vidgigal
in Rio de Janeiro ...*

A look back on my school days reveals that this time of my life was just as carefree as my childhood was. Unlike other children, I enjoyed going to school. I was (and still am) always curious and eager for knowledge.

At school and at home I always wanted to know about everything, which made the words "who, what, when, where and why" part of my daily vocabulary.

## All Kinds Of People

My first six years of school were spent at Lincoln School. I still remember my time at Lincoln School fondly, because many of the friends I made there are still my friends today, and these friendships are just as strong and sincere now as they were then – simply glorious. But I not only saw those friends at school.

*Fortunately, we also all lived in the same neighbourhood, so it was easy for us to spend time together and have fun after school. Just recently, this school was renamed "Dionne Warwick Institute" in my honour, which is the most wonderful indication of appreciation for me as a person that I have ever been fortunate enough to experience, and an honour I will certainly never forget.*

— · ⚜ · —

## Are You There

*After Lincoln School, I went to Vernon L. Davey Jr. High School (V.L.D.) for the seventh and eighth grades. There I felt for the first time a certain feeling of independence, just as every maturing student does at some point. Just riding the bus to school, buying my own lunch in the school cafeteria – that gave us teenagers a feeling of responsibility and trust. It helped us to grow up. When I think back, it seems time just flew by.*

*We went from one class to the next, were able to join various clubs, and yet we were constantly busy preparing for high school. And like a real american teenager, I was also a cheerleader, sang in the choir (no matter which school I happened to be in at the time), played on the badminton and tennis teams – to make a long story short, we exercised our bodies and minds, and we were always rewarded for our performance.*

*... and me*

*Singing in the choir was always my favourite activity by far. It was the greatest feeling for me when I was accepted into the "All-State-Choir". To be accepted into the "All-State-Choir", you had to audition, then participate in a contest. Just making the preliminary cut was a huge honour. The selection process was long and not easy. First the high school music department recommended certain students to take part in the contest. From the students on this list, the high school principal and the director of the music department then chose the ones who were actually allowed to participate. For me, it was an incredibly marvelous event, because there was only a limited number of openings, and you got to sing with the very best singers in the state. The final concert was held in Atlantic City, a glorious moment that I will never forget.*

*After Vernon L. Davey Jr. High School, I attended the ninth to twelfth grades at East Orange High School (E.O.H.S.). There we were able to make full use of all the things we had learned from elementary school to junior high school. And that was as it should have been, because high school challenged us to the fullest and required all of our acquired knowledge. In addition - and this is what I loved and admired most about my school days - we had room to dream. I never once had the feeling that my thoughts were limited.*

## I Concentrate On You

*During my school days, we were given the chance to truly advance ourselves with the things we learned, and to move up in the world. That way I was privileged to learn something that is no longer entirely true in today's world: if you work hard in school, you can achieve your goals and make your dreams come true ! When we graduated from college, we were doctors, lawyers, teachers, scientists, government employees, actors and actresses and - entertainer. Who would have thought it ?*

As a little girl, I never had the slightest notion that I would one day be in this profession. Like most girls, I wanted to be all sorts of things while I was growing up. One of my first dream jobs was court stenographer.

Back then, I thought that must be a very interesting job, because it would give me access to the courtroom and various court cases. That seemed pretty thrilling and exciting to me. Another time it was the teaching profession that went through my head. The appeal of that job was being able to "share" things with others. That in itself was fascinating to me.

*You Are The Top*

And then for a while it was the vocation of ballet dancer that seemed to me to be the most dignified of all. And to this day I love to see artists moving elegantly on stage. Even for me, good posture is the most important thing of all, especially during my concerts. I wasn't able to become a ballet dancer, but I did take ballet classes, which helped me move graciously and properly on stage.

„*I am very proud of my daughter for many reasons.*

*She has become the lady that I hoped she would be.*

*and for the many wonderful things*

*that she has done for so many.*"

*Lee Warrick*

*My Schooldays Were Carefree*

*Special Olympics (U.S. Open Tennis 2000)*

# Father

# God

or the beautiful idea

that should accompany

us throughout

our lives

*All too often in life, we find ourselves in situations in which we think there is no way out. But in these moments we pity ourselves too much, and forget that we have a "Good Father" who is always at our side. This "Good Father" is God and it is he and none other whose very existence is intended to make it clear to us that there is always a solution for even the most apparently hopeless of situations, and that even seemingly immutable patterns can ultimately be changed with ease.*

## Humbly I Pray

*The fact that God really exists and that he – even if we don't always notice it – is always with us, can be seen even in the little things of life. The very fact that we can wake up each morning, that we can shape each day according to our wishes, demonstrates his existence.*

*Indeed, his existence among us cannot be overlooked: trees, flowers, animals, human beings, storms, rain, snow, sunshine and many other things are proof that God resides among us. In essence: everything we are permitted to see, feel, touch, smell and eat derives from God's existence. If we learn to recognise God in all these forms of expression, we will always be surrounded by the feeling that even what seems impossible is in fact possible.*

*The Bible – the Word of God – can offer valuable support in learning to recognise God, but it is in no way an instruction manual, and the Bible should not be read like a normal book. I personally read the Bible as a source of comfort in both happy and sad times. For me, it is a book that teaches me how I should deal with myself and others at such times.*

*The Bible has an answer for everything, and I am certain I could recommend suitable Bible passages to a person in a particular emotional situation. However, it is up to each individual to decide whether they want to accept the Bible as a guide, or place their trust in the Bible.*

*I personally am totally convinced that all of us– the living and the dead – will gather together somewhere someday, and when that time arrives, I am looking forward most of all to seeing one special person: my friend Jesus.*

*When I was a young girl, I was taught that he was chosen by God to prepare the way for God into the hearts of all people on earth, and that he had proven to non believers again and again the existence of his father. In my eyes, he was a normal man who was prepared to solve the problems of this world, with the power and the will of God. In the end, he paid with his life the price of his faith, but in so doing protected the life of humankind from the wrath of God over the misguided conditions on earth.*

*It would be wonderful if we could extract power and energy not only from the big things in life, but also – despite the stress and hectic pace of our daily routine – see the little, inconspicuous everyday phenomena as a source of strength and as evidence for the existence of God. I believe that doing so can make our lives more pleasant and less complicated for us on a number of levels.*

**I Say A Little Prayer For You**

Professional Experience

*or the good fortune*

*to be in the right place*

*at the right time*

*my birthday party in Los Angeles*

„*I wish for Dionne all that she wants*

*in this world and the best health and good fortune !*"

*Jeffrey Lewis*

me and Aldo Luongo

*I never cease to be amazed at myself when I look back on my professional career. Is there anything in the world that is better than doing what you love to do most, every day for forty years? I don't think I need to use words about the happiness my singing has brought to me – it is a gift of God.*

❦

*On the one hand, mine was a difficult path, especially at the beginning of my career, and I had to find my way across the vast landscape of the music world. Back in the days of my first performances, there were many good singers around the world, and soon after my first attempts on stage it became clear to me that the music industry is a place where the competition never sleeps, and where one must stand up and be counted (with a lot of perseverance).*

## Do You Know The Way To S.J.

duett session in L.A.,
Ivan Lins and me

Congressman
Donald Payne
and me ...

... and Senator Ted Kennedy

*On the other hand, I never really worried about my future as a singer, because I believe in God and know that God has a plan for each of us, and also for me. If you adopt this attitude, I believe success is possible for each and every one of us, because with God, we have been given the ability to achieve it.*

*The ability to create one's own success gives rise to another ability God has given us. Each of us has been given talents that we develop in the course of our lives, potential that we should take full advantage of. Of course, some people are more talented than others, but ultimately, the important thing is whether we discover those talents, and how we express them to our environment and fullest potential.*

"Cheese", Gladys Knight

Unfortunately in the music industry, the success of a song is often measured in record sales and the length of time it stays on the national or international charts. But success – and successful experiences - cannot be categorized into "small" and "large". In my eyes, being successful is like receiving a tremendous gift.

I am personally very grateful that success came to me gradually according to my abilities, so that I was able to accept it, learn to appreciate it and enjoy it in stages. But it is important to learn to appreciate not only each success we achieve and earn, but also what remains of success, because success never lasts forever, it dissipates with time. That is a lesson every artist should learn, because otherwise they are in danger of losing themselves in the peaks and valleys of success.

Lamar White and me

## The April Fools

*"Surprise", me and Hillary Clinton*

*Manny Davis Jr. (Sammys Son) and me*

*Success is unpredictable: it can overwhelm a person like the waves of the ocean, or it can come, as it did in my case, in gradual doses spread out over forty years. I am glad that success came piece by piece in my career, because that way I was able to learn to deal with those "peaks" and "valleys".*

*Because success cannot be measured and because it has to do with a person's emotions, it's difficult to say – when I look back at the past decades – which successes meant more to me than others. And because one wonderful success followed the other, I can't separate them from one another !*

*Lena and me (at Lena Horne's Award Party)*

*Milton Berle and me*

## Walk On By

*Of tremendous importance to me are the "moving moments" that I experience in my profession, and which are an essential part of any success.*

———— ⚜ ————

*When I see the care the technicians take to ensure that my appearance onstage goes smoothly, when I hear the audience singing along in my concerts (especially in countries where they don't even speak my language), when I feel the audience's love for me and their appreciation for what I do, when as on numerous occasions I have received awards for doing what I love doing most, namely singing – all this forms the tremendously important foundation without which I would not be where I am today, and without which I would have had no success at all.*

Beverly Johnson and me

## Be My Neighbour

"I am the first !",
me and Paul Mooney

*the "Greatest": Isaac Hayes*

*Burt Bacharach, Lee Warrick, Clive Davis, me, Hal David and my son David Elliott*

*"Come into my arms !",*
*me and Elizabeth Lands*

## Moments Aren´t Moments

*Success can disappear as quickly as it comes. I was particularly fortunate in my career because many of my friends have also been active in the music industry for many years. These friendships still exist today, and they are still just as strong as friendships I have maintained since my young school days.*

❧

*It may seem bewildering that I refer to my professional colleagues as "friends". Maybe it sounds strange, but it's true ! In fact, we are a "family", because we treat each other like a real family. We help each other in good times and in bad, we spend a lot of time together, we are preoccupied with each others' future, we take an interest in one another's life and career, and we attend various festivities together, such as weddings, birthdays and births. It all sounds pretty "normal", doesn't it ?*

*In addition, throughout the years I have always been blessed with the uninterrupted support of my family and circle of friends. Their faith in me as a person, and their encouragement - it's impossible to imagine anything more beautiful.*

*There are always dry spells, and of course there were times in my life when I wanted to give up my profession entirely. It was during the "disco craze", a period when my records were no longer being bought or played. This situation took a heavy toll on my nerves, and I wanted to leave the music business.*

*Today I'm glad that I didn't act on those thoughts. Fortunately, Clive Davis simply said to me: "You may be ready to give the industry up, but the industry is not ready to give up on you." Who knows what would have happened if I had never heard these words ?*

*Confidence and self-esteem I got from my family and friends, and I have tried to use wisely. These two emotions are extremly important in the entertainment industry, especially when it comes to maintaining a certain image. Image is extremely important throughout the entire span of a career in the entertainment industry.*

## Stay Devoted

*Danny Devito and me*

Philip Michael Thomas

As far as "image maintenance" is concerned, I have always separated my professional from my private life. I would go so far as to say that that was the best path, both for me and for my family. One's private life must remain "private", this I firmly believe. Of course, I have always recognized my duty to present my talents and skills to the audience to the best of my ability during my performances.

In fact, I would even say: I owe my talent to the audience. The best thanks for the talent I display as an entertainer is when I see a smile on the faces of the audience, and when I am able with my songs to give a little moment of joy to the people who visit my concerts. My goal was always to give the audience - regardless of where I was performing - a few hours of joy. In turn, the audience gave me applause as an indication of their appreciation of my profession and the joy my songs provided.

another time,
Gladys Knight
and me

*"We Are The World" (Grammy Award): Quincy Jones, me, Michael Jackson, Stevie Wonder and Lionel Richie*

*"photo session" with Bill Graham*

Whether in my private life or in my professional life, I believe maintaining a private sphere has something to do with mutual respect: just as I respect the privacy of those who visit my concerts, I want the audience to respect mine. I am a "human being", just as sensitive and fragile as any other person.

The method of dealing with success I mentioned above, and the maintenance of one's image, are not simply second nature to artists. I myself worked very hard on myself and my reputation for years in order to be what I wanted to be, the person I still am today.

## Begin The Beguine

*me and Julius "Dr.J" Irving*

Burt Bacharach and me in Tokyo

Natalie Cole, Isaac Hayes and me

## Get A Kick Out Of You

*Lionel Richie and me*

*Gladys Knight,*
*Philip Michael Thomas,*
*his nephew James and me*

*Even now, I work hard on myself, in order to represent those things for which my audience has come to know and appreciate me. It's hard work, I can assure you. But in the end, all the toil and effort have been worthwhile. I'm proud of the results: the Dionne Warwick of then is the Dionne Warwick of today.*

——— ❧ ———

*Decisions that I make are always taken in relation to my past career. But I do not distinguish between "difficult" and "easy" decisions, because every decision is in itself important if it influences the future of a career. Even a decision regarding which song to sing in a concert, and which not to sing, is of tremendous importance for one's image.*

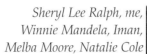

*Sheryl Lee Ralph, me,*
*Winnie Mandela, Iman,*
*Melba Moore, Natalie Cole*

*Louis Gossett Jr. and*
*Winnie Mandela*

*me and Winnie Mandela*

*Parliment Delegation from*
*Ghana / West Africa*

„When I was born, she named me
'Barrance D. Warrick'.
The 'D' stands for Dionne
and Dede (my other aunt)."


Barry Warrick

*Iman, Senator Diane Watson,*
*Nancy Wilson, Winnie Mandela and me*

*Of course, I would always prefer to sing all my songs in every show, but that idea is absurd. Especially when I'm planning a new show it's difficult for me to make a decision about which songs to sing.*

*But ultimately I choose the songs that have been well received over the past forty years and the ones the audience expects of Dionne Warwick. However, for reasons of my own, I also always include a few less-popular songs in my concerts, songs that weren't necessarily big hits, but were suddenly well received in a particular show, for whatever reason. At moments like these, I love the effect of surprise the audience gives me.*

"He is a man, she is a woman !", Isaac Hayes

*lovely Patti Labelle*

## I´ve Got You Under My Skin

*Randy Crawford and me*

## Odds & Ends

*small talk with Diahann Caroll*

I was quick to learn to deal with the phenomenon of "criticism". Criticism in general can't hurt, particularly if it's constructive. However, criticism can be delivered in such a way as to virtually "destroy" people instead of helping them along. Surely everyone knows – especially in the music industry – what I mean by "destroy". Fortunately, up to now, purely "destructive" criticism has never gained the upper hand in my career.

Generally, I don't like to advise young people on how to get into the music industry, because the industry has changed so drastically. Star search type shows are just updated versions of shows like this that have been arround for as long as I can remember. Shows like "Ted Mack" or "The Arthur Godfrey Show" name that tune, and the list goes on.

*Suzanne Pleshette, Harry Finley and me*

Gladys Knight was a winner on the "Ted Mack" show, so these shows can and do produce talented people who go on to become major stars.

The desire and preparation is really what is needed not only for a musician but for any profession. As the saying goes "when opportunity knocks, you must be ready when you open the door". Since the trend today has become that of marketable and development of kids (see all the boy groups), and the age group that is being targeted are from 9 to 18 (usually girls) is now considered the "norm".

Unfortunately, the issue of talent first is not the first thought. Time and an enormous amount of money are the priorities. Finally, when enough time and money is put into an artist (i.e. videos, print ads, billboards) and the general public is getting this as a constant diet the end results are what we have today.

*Lola Falana and me*

*"The Pointer Sisters"*

## How Long

*Mira Waters and me*

However, I must say every now and then a true talent can and will emerge. The only thing I know is that it takes a lot of dedication and self-sacrifice to be good in this job. I wish all young people, who want to prove themselves in the area of music and entertainment, plenty of endurance, because it is essential in this business.

As for me, I intend to stay in the business for a few more years, because I enjoy it. In this connection, I'd like to relate a little anecdote: a friend once asked me how it feels to be able to conjure up a moment of happiness for the people who visit my concerts, to put a smile on their faces and he asked:"Isn't it incredible ?" and I said: "Yes, it is incredible to know you've been a part of the smile times in their lives."

## Aquarela Do Brazil

*Brock Peters, Linda Hopkins,*
*Melba More and me*

74

*Sacha Distel and me (recording session in Paris)*

"Lets sing a song, Stevie Wonder !"

*Bobby Hatfield, me and Bill Medley*

*me and Barry Manilow*

*Leslie Uggams, "Little" Lena, Lena Horne*

*When Dionne called me*

*to go on tour with her,*

*she wasn't sure that I lived*

*in San Jose, California.*

*Once I gave her my address,*

*she asked*

*'Do you know the way, baby ?'"*

*Vel Lewis*

Lisa Stansfield and me

Julio Iglesias, singing duets with me

me, Diana Ross ...

*„My personal wish for Dionne is that she has everything that she wants in life."*

*Barry*

.... and Kenny Rogers

## That´s What Friends Are For

„*I wish Dionne peace,*

*perfect health and happiness !*"

*Todd Hunter*

*me, Mr. & Mrs. Montalban*
*and Harry Finley*

*my friend Sonny Bono and me*

## Always Something There

*"Dinner for 2",
Frank Sinatra
and me*

„*I always loved
Dionne's voice and
the music she sang."*

*Kathy Rubbillo*

*one of my birthday parties, Aldo Luongo, Roberta Flack, Lena Horne, Quincy Jones*

me, Glen Campbell, ...

... Lee
Majors
(New Years
Eve Party)

... and "the queen", Aretha Franklin

... Ron Kass,
Joan Collins

*"I love Paris in the summer", me and Sacha Distel (the Olympia Theatre, Paris)*

*Lee Majors and me (New Years Eve Party)*

*Nancy Sinatra, Bobby Sherman and me (Grammy Award)*

83

*Princess Margaret, Marty Feldman, me and Andy Williams at the Royal Command Performance*

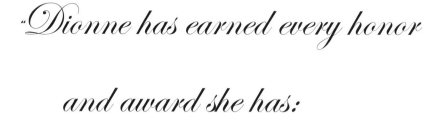

*"Dionne has earned every honor and award she has: she is the ultimate survivor!"*

*David Krause*

*Queen Mother, Marty Feldmann and me*

*me and Queen Elizabeth*

*"I am happy !", Paul Cantor and Conrad Hilton*

*No question that my mom*

*helped mold my personality.*

*Like her,*

*I 'don't take no mess !'.*

*Our family pride*

*ourselves on honesty.*

*We always have and always will. "*

*Damon*

*Neil Amstrong, his wife, and me*

*Chris Jonz, Leslie Uggams, me, Sid Barnes and Joe Fleishman*

Leslie Uggams,
Lonnie Shorr
and me

"Luther Vandross, say hello to my friends !"

„*It is important to share*

*things with my sister*

*because we think alike*

*on many fronts,*

*and we know it's a give*

*and take between us.* "

*Delia Warrick*

*Pearl Bailey and me (Fords Theatre)*

*"Thanks for your great songs, Burt."* (Burt Bacharach)

„ *She is a great performer and*

*her music is some of the best ever written !* "

*Todd Hunter*

# Forever

# On The Go

*and finding myself*

*by allowing creativity*

*free reign*

*Singing the National Anthem at an "Oakland Raiders Game"*

„The one event that I will always remember

is our performing together at the Apollo Theatre

in New York.


The song we sang was

'United We Stand, Divided We Fall',

showing our strong unity."


Delia Warrick

My life hasn't really changed after forty years in the entertainment industry. I still do concert tours as always, and am on the road a lot. There's no room in the life I lead for any kind of "daily routine", as some people might call it, because I'm always moving around and every day is different. Sometimes I find myself doing nothing but packing suitcases for days at a time: pack, unpack, pack, unpack !

Other days it seems I spend all my time trying to get from one place to another. There are days in my life when twenty-four hours just aren't enough for everything I have to do, but there are also days that stretch out and never seem to end. However, such days are a luxury for me, and I'm glad there are days like these in my life.

"I love to be onstage !"

*"Thank you, wonderful audiences all over the world."*

*"Ready for working !",*
*Arif Mardin and me*
*(Cole Porter Session)*

*„I met Dionne while doing the*
*„Colors of Christmas Tour'.*

*We became friends and*

*she asked me to join her band."*

*Jeffrey Lewis*

*Edu Lobo and his son,*
*Duet "To Say Goodbye"*

*me and Johnny Mathis*
*(Radio City)*

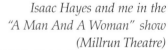

## Be Proud Of Your Heritage

*Isaac Hayes and me in the*
*"A Man And A Woman" show*
*(Millrun Theatre)*

*By the way, the word "luxury" has but one meaning to me: on those days I can really "be myself" and do whatever I feel like doing, even if that means doing nothing. That's why, whenever anyone asks me about my greatest dream outside of my profession, I always answer: "One whole day of which I don't have to make any decisions, answer any telephones, solve any problems or even take the car out of the garage !"*

*I spend a lot of my time on airplanes. They play an important role in my professional life, and for me, they are the only way to get where I am going in the quickest possible way. I can't imagine how I could do my tours without them. Of course I would be happy to travel from concert to concert by train, but unfortunately it's impossible for me, because I usually have a concert in one country on one day and in another country on the next.*

*"Dionne has*

*a great stage presence*

*which is wonderful to watch."*

*Jeffrey Lewis*

*the Vienna Boys Choir and*
*the Director of the TV-Show "Christmas in Vienna"*

*"It was always a wish*

*to perform with her.*

*Vel Lewis*

*me and John Williams,*
*"Valley Of The Dolls"*
*(recording session)*

102

*„I always enjoyed listening*

*to Dionne's songs*

*while growing up*

*and loved her style. "*

*Vel Lewis*

Joe Mele

*... another time "in concert"*

*Luther Vandross,*
*"You're kidding,*
*aren't you ?"*

*"Finally, Luther.*
*Thank you !"*
*(Hero Awards)*

*"Come to me, business man !",*
*Hal David and me*

*"You too, Marc ?*
*Congratulations,*
*Mr. Anthony !"*

105

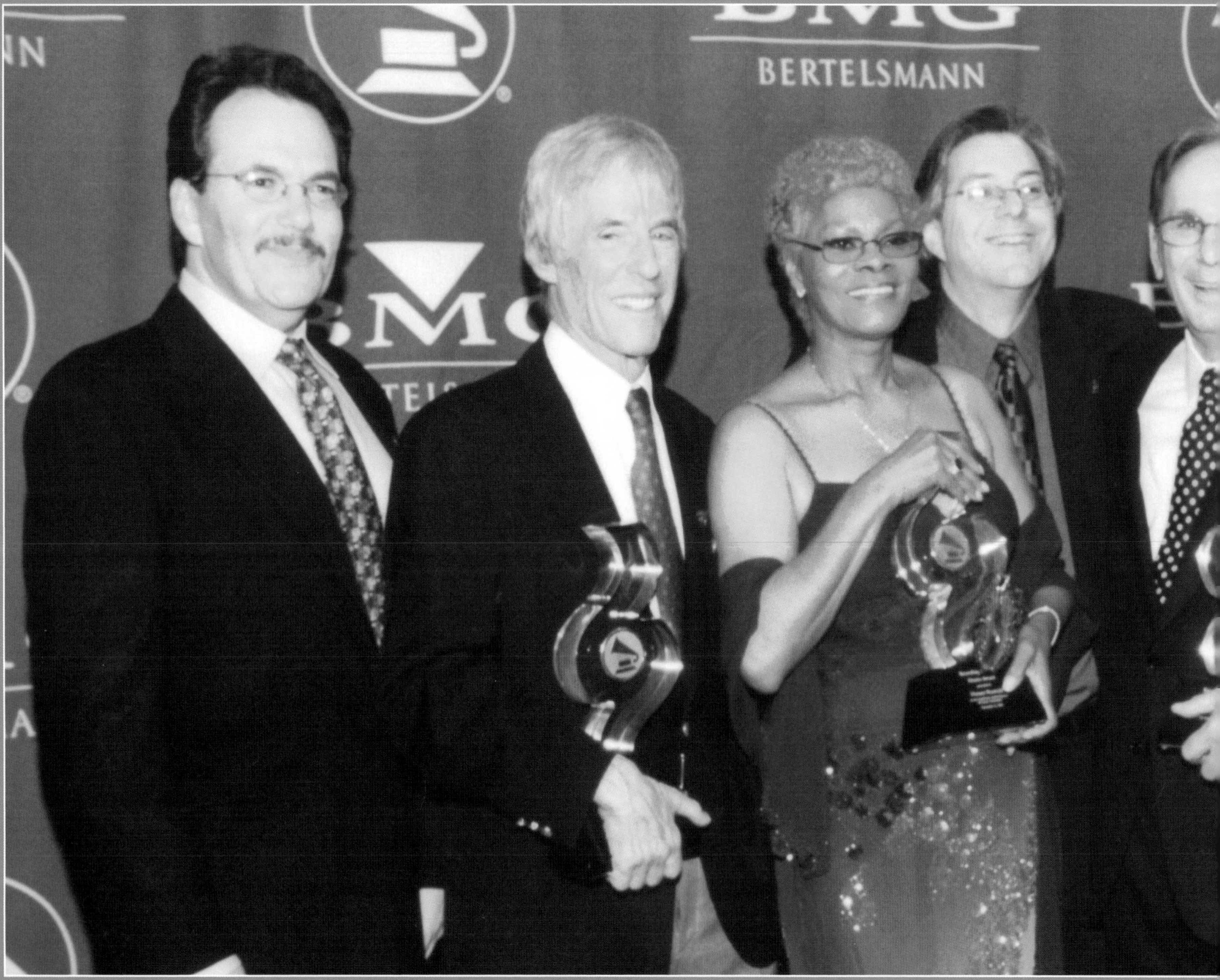
BMG
BERTELSMANN

Burt Bacharach, me
and Hal David
(Hero Awards)

„*Before I met her,*
*Dionne was already*
*considered a living legend*
*and a ‚musician's singer'.*"

*Wade Short*

*my friend Eliana in Brazil*

*my friend Teo and me
working in Brazil*

*the best background
group at the brazilian session*

## *Paper Mache*

"Breaking A Keg Of Wine" ( Tokyo Music Festival)

"Thank you for this
wonderful invitation,
Placido !" (Christmas in Vienna)

„I learned from Dionne

to listen to the music and

play from your heart."

Jeffrey Lewis

*me, my son David, my sister Delia, my son Damon, my friend Pam and mommy (Walk of Fame, L.A.)*

*"Sleeping in" is a foreign expression to me when I'm on tour. But the reason I get so little sleep is not so much that I give concerts in so many different cities and have to hurry from one place to the next without a long break. Rather, it is because I am "nosey". I don't want to miss a thing, no matter where I am in this world.*

*When I'm able to spend a few days at home in New Jersey, I enjoy it tremendously. After arriving from the airport, I can usually be found at my mother's house, basically because I don't get to see her or my sister as frequently as I'd like, but also because my mother is an unbelieveable cook. I would even venture to say she is the best cook in the world.*

*My favourite dish is her "chicken and dumplings" and I could eat this every day. I love spending time with my mother, exchanging thoughts with her. Often, we have so much to say to each other that the time between my concerts is never long enough. After visiting my mother, it's my friends' turn. Fortunately, many of my friends live in the neighbourhood, so it's no problem for us to visit one another and tell each other what's new in our lives. It is always very exciting to hear what has gone on in my absence.*

*Yours*

Joe Smith, me
and Thom Bell

„My personal wish for Dionne

is that she release a cd for her

40th anniversary in this business

and continue to enjoy

an outstanding,

legendary career."

Vel Lewis

*"Do they really know what they have to do ?"*

*I love singing*

*After reading this, many of you must be thinking that my life consists of nothing but concert tours punctuated by short visits home. Not at all !*

*As long as I can remember, I have had a "business sense" and felt that there was more to me than my talent for singing. With this in mind I created a skin care line "Enyo", a fragrance and an interior design group. I am thoroughly convinced that every person has more than one talent, and we should not be shy about sharing our talents with those around us. Until now, only a few people were aware of my talents (other than singing), but I think that will change soon – perhaps through the publication of this book.*

*The idea for my "Dionne" perfume came to me in the late seventies. Of course, it's difficult to offer a precise description of its qualities (especially if you don't know it yet). Most ask "what does your fragrance smell like ?", and to answer I say always "it is in the oriental family of fragrances as is Obsession, Oscar and Shalimar."*

*Sacha Distel, me
and Mireille Mathieu in Paris*

*my marvelous production manager*

Before creating "Dionne", I was so wild about Shalimar, I bought it in huge quantities. I could have opened an entire shop just to sell all the bottles of Shalimar I had collected. But then came the time when I thought to myself: "With all the money I kept spending on Shalimar, I could just as easily create a perfume of my own !"

No sooner said than done. That was the birth of the sweet, soft and very sensual scent called "Dionne", which includes a bath gelee and a moisturizing lotion.

The following concept also sounds a little strange the first time one hears about it. Still, after trying out a variety of cosmetic products, I noticed that there weren't many really good skin care products developed especially for women of colour. Before long, I went to work to fill this incredible gap and I created a special skin care regimen called "Enyo".

*Renato Braza*
*singing outdoor with me in Chicago*

117

*"Laughing is the best medicine !"*
*(Sammy Davis Jr. Telethon)*

Seventeen years ago, at a cocktail party for interior design, I met Bruce Garrick (who is now my partner) and his business partner at the time, an architect named Bob Cheroski, who has since unfortunately passed away. We happened to strike up a conversation and after a little while told each other our reasons for visiting the party in the first place. The two of them were already quite experienced in the interior design industry.

Bruce and Bob asked me if I would like to help them on one of their projects and this is how it all began. Today, Bruce and I are the DWDG (Dionne Warwick Design Group) and we already have designed many homes and offices. I'm confident that we are capable of fulfilling the most individualised wishes of our clients. We feel we have the ability to fulfill the needs and desires of our clients, and making "dreams come true". We usually work at Bruce's house, out in the middle of the desert.

*children, the show was benefiting,*
*"I got you, kids !"*

*my cousin Felicia*
*and me…*

## Wives And Lovers

*… in action*

*Congressman Charles Rangel, me, Luther Vandross and the Director of the "Harlem Renaissance Program"*

## Another Night

*While it's true I'm more a "city person" than a "child of the desert", the barren atmosphere of the desert seems to me the perfect place to allow one's creativity to run free. Besides, Palm Desert is not far from Los Angeles and San Francisco, cities where we have steady customers and reliable colleagues.*

*As you can see, I keep busy. But all the tasks I've been telling you about here are tremendous fun and one-hundred percent fulfilling. In spite of all the traveling and the many decisions I'm constantly called upon to take, I don't feel worn out, but well balanced; not run down, but full of energy.*

*I would like to recommend the following to each of you: do everything you can to make the very most of your own personal talents. I would be very happy if I, by describing my own way of life, could bring home to others how wonderful it is for one's own ego to live out one's talents to the fullest, and to allow others to share and enjoy these talents.*

„*My personal wish*

*for Dionne*

*is that she*

*has everything*

*that she wants in life.*"

*Barry Warrick*

*"Do you know
my songs ?"
(Radio City)*

Luther Vandross

*„I like to be on stage with her because of the consistant high level of performance required and the fantastic musicality of her performances."*

*Wade Short*

## The Windows Of The World

*Sir Elton John, me,
Gladys Knight and
Stevie Wonder*

## I Promise You

*"Big hugs !", Howard Hewett and me*

„*I have learned from Dionne*

*that you don't bet what you don't earn.*

*She always gives 100 % on stage –*

*people never know if she has had a bad day.*"

*David Krause*

*my appointment to "Ambassador of Health"*

„*I wish for Dionne*

*that she continues to be recognised*

*for her great musical and*

*humanitarian achievements and*

*for her own happiness.*"

*Wade Short*

*Jack, Barbara,*
*Henry, Donjo and me*
*(Scholarship Foundation /*
*Pinochle Tournament - Benefit)*

*"Jay Bernstein Awards Dinner"*
*Jay Bernstein, me and Stacey Keach*

*party in Tokyo, Burt Bacharach and me*

*„Before I knew Dionne, she*

*was a classy lady*

*and a marvelous performer.*

*making some jokes during recording session*

*My parents always listened to Dionne,*

*so it was a dream to play with her. "*

*Jeffrey Lewis*

*Déjà Vu*

# My Wishes

# And I

*or nostalgia for*

*the good old days*

me and "Dionne"(another christmas party)

„*I like to share jokes*

*with my sister, although she*

*doesn't tell jokes*

*as well as I do,*

*its all about a 'chuckle'!*"

*Delia Warrick*

*Look at my wonderful tree*

*The best thing that can happen to me each day is being able to wake up in the morning.*

*My first thoughts of the day are dedicated to thanking God for this privilege. Then I throw back the covers, make myself a cup of coffee (if I'm at home) and look out the window to see what Mother Nature is up to.*

*I've already given you an indication of what my day can look like. But what makes Dionne Dionne – that is, how I see myself – will be the subject of this chapter.*

## The Woman That I Am

*"Christmas forever !"*

It's not at all easy for me to describe myself. Because my personality contains so many components of my ancestors, especially my parents, it's difficult for me to say what is really purely "Dionne".

I valued honesty even as a child. Over the years, I have had to learn that not many people want to have anything to do with honesty, and that people sometimes get places faster with dishonesty than they do with honest behaviour.

Nevertheless, I have never let others' actions influence me. One reason for that may be that I was born under the sign of Sagittarius, a fire sign, which means that I am quite frank and tell people what I think.

dancing Samba in Rio

## Say Always: I Love You !

„If I had the chance to look through

my moms eyes, I would know

I'd be proud of how my sons

have grown up to mimic the  skills

and positive influence I have given them,

and hope they pass on the skills for life  on to their children."

Damon

Some Changes Are For Good

*one of my birthdays, "I had a ball!"*

„ *What I have learned*

*from my mom*

*is priceless !"*

*Damon*

Contrary to what many people believe, I have also enjoyed, for as long as I can remember, being influenced by others. In my opinion, being "influenced" shouldn't carry such a negative connotation, because this process of being influenced can bring "fruitful" results for a person.

Outside of my profession, I am often influenced by people and things, and this influence positively enriches my life. Among them are my mother especially, as well as my relatives, my friends and my children.

They all influence me in many different ways, and they are so incredibly motivating that they always keep me on my toes, no matter what I am doing.

*Delia Warrick, my sister*

*A House Is Not A Home*

*wonderful trip in Abudabi Arabia*

*My strong point, as I have said, is honesty. One of my weaknesses is that I can't say "no". I don't know why that is, but I believe I simply don't want to hurt anyone. On the other hand, it's difficult for me to keep my daily schedule under control.*

*I do love my work, and everything I have been able to do (and not do) over the past forty years, but from time to time things seem to pile up on me and knock me off balance. It sometimes takes hours or even days before I can get things back in order. For this reason, I could never offer anyone advice about how best to plan for a day's work, because it's something I have trouble with myself.*

*I am very proud of my heritage and my skin colour. I'm proud to be an African American. I would be very happy if I in the field of entertainment – like others in the areas of science, education, art, music or law – could inspire the young generation of blacks to follow in my footsteps and carry on our heritage.*

## Our Day Will Come

*my lovely Cheyenne (Halloween Party)*

*that's me, in Aspen (Colorado)*

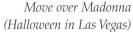

# Then Came You

*Move over Madonna (Halloween in Las Vegas)*

*Whenever I hear the word "minority" used in the media in connection with blacks or people of colour, I never feel like they are addressing me, Dionne Warwick. Indeed, I believe there is still much to discuss about the word "minority", regardless of whom we are referring to as a "minority". It's not just that the definition of the word "minority" is insufficient in my eyes. No, in the worldwide discussion of this strange and man-made phenomenon, it's never really about how the use of this concept can be avoided in the first place.*

*I myself have, thank God, never experienced discrimination because of my appearance, and I would hope people could realise that there are more important things in life than creating differences between ourselves. And that brings me once again to my "wish list".*

141

*at a benefit party for scholarship*

*I think about a lot of things while going about my job. In my eyes, people should turn back the history of our species a bit. We are not in this world to spread war, destruction and disease. We are in this world to love each other, to care for each other and to take care of our bodies. Humanity is what is important, and we should acknowledge this point much more often.*

## Alfie

*I was never cut out for politics, and that's why I'm not interested in politics. In fact, I consider it a waste of time to think about political things, especially when the fundaments of our society are no longer in harmony. I think it makes much more sense to visit foreign countries and learn about their cultures.*

*Henry, me, David and Cheyenne in San Diego*

*"I cannot stop my tears.", receiving a gold album (Carnegie Hall)*

„*I continue to learn from my experiences in traveling with Dionne. She is a good example of someone who is able to maintain grace while under the pressures of being on the road."*

*Todd Hunter*

*Darlene, me, Edna and Delia*

*Guy making jokes*

During my own travels, I have had the marvelous opportunity to truly understand other countries and customs, not only by observing them, but because I have also always paid heed to the respective customs, accepted and experienced them.

## Captives Of The Heart

As a result I have been better able to understand the way of life of people who live outside of the United States. This is what I call "cross-cultural communication", the best way to do away with prejudice. In this context, the United States of America are another example for international understanding. The USA is an example for how the principle of the melting pot can work. So many different kinds of people from various nations live in this country, and they have not only chosen it as their home, they also want to get along with one another. And as we can see: it works.

*Since my vision of life is based on the principle of hope, I would very much like to see a world in which peace reigns, where children never hunger and where the family, as a symbol of our common survival, is once again placed at the centre of society.*

*Children should be children again, and be allowed to enjoy their childhood to the fullest. If all this could happen, we would once again live as we used to, without problems and concerns. Today, in many ways, I miss the "good old days".*

*But, with a little effort, a little common sense and the power of the Lord, we can regain what has been lost and make the impossible possible. I'm thoroughly convinced of it !*

*relaxing position*

# My Wonderful Family

*or the joys*

*of motherhood*

Mancel Warrick

„*She was named after my sister, Marie, and my husbands cousin who was also her god mother.*"

*Lee Warrick*

*mommy*

Love Will Find A Way

*daddy*

„*I consider Dionne an adult,*

*however, she will always be my 'child', although*

*she is an adult with children*

*and grandchildren on her own.*"

*Lee Warrick*

**Take The Short Way Home**

*mommy and me*

*Whenever I talk about my childhood, it is so easy. I love to remember how life treated Dionne at different ages: as an innocent little baby, as a small child and of course as a teenager.*

*I was born in Orange and grew up in East Orange (New Jersey). We, that is my mother, my father, my sister, my brother and I, lived on Sterling Street. My brother and sister and I didn't move out until after we had finished high school.*

*My childhood was quite normal. My relationship with my parents and grandparents was one of love, and care for as long as I can remember.*

„Brothers and sisters will always have

an important role in our lives. You have one mother,

one father, and siblings

that you can always depend upon.

Blood will always be thicker than water,

insofar as I am concerned."

Delia Warrick

The Beginning Of Loneliness

## They Long To Be Close To You

Delia and mommy

My father, who unfortunately is no longer with us, worked for many years as a pullman porter. Then one day he decided he wanted to change jobs, so he bought a small candy store and soda parlor near our house, and finally became a merchant.

His leisure-time activities were incredibly diverse. He loved fishing and hunting, going to baseball games and playing cards with his friends.

156

„*I just feel love,*

*love, love and*

*more love.*"

*Damon*

*on the way to Rome, Willie and me*

*my husband Bill Elliott, me, with nephew Barry Warrick and son David at the circus*

„*My entire childhood was amazing. Growing up was like*

*a fairytale. My mom provided the perfect existence*

*for me and my brother.*"

*David Elliott*

My mother on the other hand, who still lives in Orange (New Jersey), used to work for an energy company named "Tung Sol" that specialized in manufacturing parts for light bulbs.

However, she was the best housewife you can imagine, always fashionable and up to date, had a good sense of style and knew how a lady should behave.

## Take Good Care Of You And Me

my son David
"I love you, mommy !"

„My mother's love for me is unconditional.

She has raised my brother and myself

in a disciplined environment full of love that has taught me

how to instill her teachings in my daughter."

Damon

Let Me Go To Him

*David, Damon ...*
*Damon, me and*
*David and again,*
*and again,*
*and again ...*

*David and Damon*

## Trains And Boats And Plains

*Brazil, new home*

*I think my mother taught me a lot in that respect, just by watching and following her example, and I'm eternally grateful to her for it.*

*Fortunately, I was one of those children who got to know their grandparents – on both my mother's and my father's side. Every moment I was able to spend with them still lives in my memory, and even today it's always a beautiful, special feeling for me when I think back on them.*

*My father's father, for example, came from Kansas and was a man of the cloth. When we were children, we spent a lot of our free time with him. He told us all the wonderful Bible stories. Afterwards we often riddled him with "whys" and "how comes" – questions that arose naturally from the stories he told. I loved sitting next to him and letting him tell me about God. I'm sure he laid the foundation for my faith when he told me that my faith in God would protect me as long as I live.*

## In Between The Heartaches

*What I learned from him about the Bible has stayed with me to this day, and I have never regretted those "lessons".*

*My father's mother, born in Alabama, taught me to knit and sew when I was about ten years old, because knitting and sewing fascinated me from the very beginning. When Grandma went into the kitchen to make dinner for all of us, I looked over her shoulder as often as I could to learn some of her cooking skills. Next to my mother, she was the second-best cook I have ever known.*

*What for many people today sounds like an idyllic scene of family life, was and still is a tradition in our family: having meals together !*

*me, Damon and a friend*

The kind of hostility among relatives that has unfortunately become so common in the twenty-first century was completely unknown to us. Our family ties were harmonious and strong. My mother's parents were very close friends of my father's parents. My mother's parents were even active members in the church my father's father pastored. That church meant everything to them.

The time I was privileged to spend with my parents and grandparents was full of moments of togetherness. This was an irreplaceable treasure to me as a child, a kind of "spiritual wealth". Whether it was summer holidays, a birthday, a picnic, a church visit or some other activity, the family stuck together, and each of us enjoyed being around each other. And that brings me to a subject that is close to my heart, and about which I feel I must speak out honestly.

*Damon, me, David and Delia*

Nate Carr and Henry, "My brothers !"

When I look at our society today, I come to the sad realization that what my family took for granted as "normal" doesn't exist anymore. People still get together to celebrate a birthday, or pay their respects to a pair of newlyweds, because they are part of the family – but it all seems like an obligation rather than something they do because they enjoy being with their family.

As many people have made their personal careers the centre of their lives, I believe the family has over the course of the past few decades forfeited much of its importance. In today's world, it almost sounds laughable when I claim that eating together as a family is important.

## How Many Times Can We Say

Johnny Mathis, Jack Elliott and me

166

Ultimately I am convinced that each individual person is distinguished by his or her own family, and that we all, both in the present and in the future, should take care to ensure that the family is restored to its place of importance in society. It is our family that shapes us, that gives us answers to the questions we grapple with all our lives.

The family is the mirror of life, a reflection of our own life, whether we want to admit it or not. Everything we do, all of our strivings, our very character – it all originates in our families and our ancestors. The sooner we recognize this simple fact, the better we can get along with ourselves as well as with our families and our fellow human beings. Once we have accepted the family as the cornerstone of our lives, we can begin to see the family as an "identity", as a "unity".

*my son Damon and his family,*
*Kaelyn, Neko and Tamani*

*Cheyenne and her first Christmas*

*Families are made up of many personalities, characters, opinions and lifestyles, all of which leave little room for perfection. "Identity" or "unity" really means "equality", it means that in our own family, and among one another, we are all the same.*

*We all share the same origins, and no one is better than anyone else. The only thing that can distinguish us within a family is the era in which we live and grow up. For example, I became mobile at a much younger age than my parents were able to when they were growing up, and my children are quicker to do many things than I was in my youth.*

## Who Is Gonna Love Me

*Cheyenne and Rio*

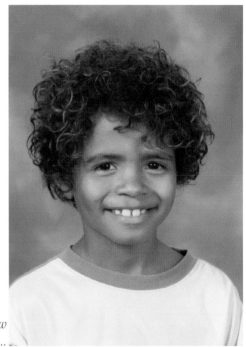

*Mandela and Maya*

*Mandela a few years later ...*

*... and Maya a few years later*

*my grandson,*
*Neko*

## Heartbreaker

*The one thing that should be a constant in a family is "unity". Everyone supports each other, in good times and in bad. Only as a unified whole do family ties remain strong. It is my personal wish that families will once again find their "unity".*

⚜

*In my family, it's easy to see that we all have the same origins. All I have to do is look at my grandchildren, and I see myself as a young child. Like me, each of my five grandchildren have their own personalities, and are interested in many things all being those things children are usually interested in. The girls playing with dolls, dressing up, playing kitchen and dance. The boys playing baseball, basketball, football, soccer and hockey. However, I'm proud of the way they are growing up and developing. The best thing for me is that I have had the pleasure of having my grands on the road with me.*

*I am confident they will all find their own way and realize their dreams. When I was growing up, my beloved grandfather – the preacher – said to me: "Baby ! If you can think it you can do it!" This sentence is so simple, and so true and the logic has been the key for me, not only in my youth, but right up to this very moment. I have passed this also on to my children and they are giving it to their children, and finally I hope all of the people will receive this message through this book.*

*Kaelyn, my granddaughter ...*

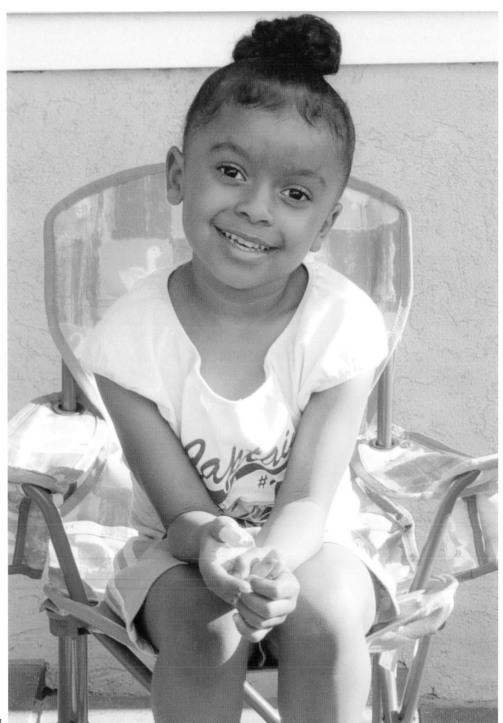

*... and again: Kaelyn*

*my cousin Whitney Houston*

*Being a mother and having a family of my own has been the most fulfilling thing in my entire life. Being a parent is such a wonderful experience. Both of my sons have made me proud since the day they were born, and they have grown up to become loving parents and generous human beings. They have also given me wondeerful grandchildren. We talk as often as possible on the phone, and we never say "Goodbye", we always end our talks with "I love you".*

*There is no instruction manual for becoming a good parent. Just as it is with personal relationships, you have to go through it yourself. In my view, it's important for parents to make clear to their children two fundamental principles while they are growing up: the principle of give and take, and the principle of sharing.*

*When our children reach a certain age, we automatically begin teaching them how important it is to give and take, and also how important it is to share. Learning these two principles is, in my opinion, the foundation children need before they can be sent out into the adult world. Many parents know that the principle of sharing is the most difficult thing their children must learn. When it comes to sharing, we usually hear children say "That's mine !" or just the word "mine".*

**This Girl´s In Love With You**

*aunt Cissy Houston*

The bottom line is that it's up to parents to teach their children that the principle of sharing only makes sense when it becomes clear that the "act of sharing" makes more than one person happy. It's like playing ball: it's not as much fun to play ball by yourself as it is to play with others. In a group, playing ball is more fun.

This may all sound like a lot of advice, but it's not intended to be. I personally would never allow myself to give advice, no matter what the subject, but I do know being a parent is a process one has to go through by one's self.

Recently I read the autobiography of Hillary Clinton, and there was a passage about "parenthood" and "motherhood" that fits well here. Hillary once said to her daughter Chelsea: "It's new for both of us. I've never been a mother before, and you were never a baby before. We just have to support each other as best we can."

## Love Begins With You

*aunt Rebie, mommy and aunt Annie*

*Whitney, Cheyenne, Bobbi Kris and Bobby*

"Family Affair", cousin Felicia, Withney, niece Deanna and nephew Barry

I think there's no better way to put it. It's up to each individual, when he or she becomes a parent, to find a way to deal with each situation and the overall process. Being a parent is both a gift and a job. The feeling of having responsibility for a little being is an indescribably beautiful one – both for a father and a mother – and at the same time quite overwhelming.

## High Upon This Love

Of course, I see the part a woman plays in the partnership with her child as a somewhat larger one than that of a man. Speaking for this mother, and all the women who are mothers, we are the nurturers of the world, the "chief cooks and bottle washers", the ones who in the final analysis provide our children and our family with comfort. In my family, there's still a prevailing attitude of "Mommy can do it !" - and to this day "Mommy" has always had a solution for every problem.

*In closing, it is my express wish that every person in the world might have as wonderful a family as the one God has given me, a family in which love and respect are the highest priorities. Even though the gift and the duties of "family" requires a lot of effort, I am thoroughly convinced that it has been more than worthwhile, as it has enriched my life!*

*„The lesson of life is*

*to do what you have to do*

*and give it your best, don't half do it."*

*Lee Warrick*

"Christmas Eve", Bobby, Whitney, Cheyenne and David

## Love At Second Sight

# Power

# Of Love

*or how it is possible*

*not to lose oneself*

*Stars turning in Droves for Gathering Place Benefit*

Pauletta and Denzel Washington were the hosts for one of the most successful fundraising events to be held this side of the annual Urban League dinner. The Washingtons hosted a black-tie reception in the home of The Honorary Chairperson, Dionne Warwick. The stars on hand to lend talents and their checkbooks to the cause of raising funds for Gathering Place, the only daytime drop-in center assisting South Central L.A. mothers and children impacted by HIV/AIDS, were too numerous to mention. The reception was the first of two events held the weekend of May 1 that included a celebrity Basketball Game at Loyola Marymount the next day. Seen here: (Top left): Brenda Russell, Denzel Washington and Chaka Khan; (Bottom left) Miki Howard, Beverly Todd and Jackee; (center) David Elliott, Dionne Warwick and Damien Elliott (Dionne's sons); (Above) Henry Carr, Denzel, Dionne, Pauletta Washington and Paul Mooney. Photos by John Davis

*Henry Carr, Denzel Washington, me, Pauletta Washington and Paul Mooney*

*Brock Peters and
Senator Diane Watson*

*Again and again in my life, I have been confronted with the "power" of love. There were moments in which it gave me strength and joy, but there were also situations in which it brought me tears and pain.*

———— ⚜ ————

*On these occasions, what helped me most was my profession as an entertainer. For example, when I was unhappy because of love, my lyrics and melodies helped me through the sad phases of my life.*

*Because love is one of those human emotions that are difficult to explain, I believe it is like motherhood or the birth of a child: You just have to be there when it happens. Indeed, you have to feel the emotion to know what all the fuss is about. Once the feeling of love is inside you, a learning process should begin as soon as possible.*

*David and
Claudette Robinson*

*Aristede, President of Haiti and me*

*For example, if you experience unrequited love, the learning process can help you avoid such disappointment in the future. Love, like so many things in life, is not an easy thing.*

*Dealing with the unpleasant aspects of love's disappointments is something people must learn for themselves. I once sang a song called "I'll Never Fall In Love Again", in which the individual verses spoke of why it's better not to fall in love.*

*"Best Friends", Mr. & Mrs. Bishop*

## Reach Out For Me

*Paul and Ronnie Cantor & Michael Travis*

Craig Stevens, Alexis Smith
and Julia at one of my
birthday parties

## Only Love Can Break A Heart

Winnie Mandela and Leslie Uggams

Of course, the song's lyrics present an extreme view, but the text is intended as encouragement to anyone who is experiencing heartache and doesn't know where to turn. I don't want to offer any tips for a good relationship.

Whether two people can live together always depends on their personality and their ability to learn. I myself probably fell in love millions of times while I was growing up.

*"Hello - Mr. Gilbert !",
(Music Teacher at E.O.H.S.)*

As an adult, I've been "attached" three times. But in all of my relationships I was privileged to learn how important it is to give your partner enough space and allow them to develop their own creativity. I also learned how important it is to say "I love you" every day ! This sentence is incredibly important, because it imparts a feeling of togetherness, pride, hope, trust and protection – very fundamental elements in a partnership. And finally, when it comes to love, another personal attitude that was very helpful to me was to admit my mistakes and to apologize for them rather than trying to hide them.

When we speak of love, we all too often think only of the kind of love involved in a partnership. But love is more than that. There is our love for God, our love for our children, our love for our family, our love for our grand-children, our love of life and many other kinds of love.

In recognition of the aforementioned fact that love is often seen in an one-dimensional way, my conclusion is: not until we learn to recognize what a valuable treasure each new day is will we realise how grateful we really should be, and how ungrateful we were before. Love plays a key role along the pathway to this understanding, and is a consequence of thankfulness. We have been placed in this world to spread love every day - in whatever form !

*"Cheers",
Bruce Garrick*

*me, Shirley and Rochelle*

„*No question that my mom helped mold my personality. Like her, I 'don't take no mess !'. Our family pride ourselves on honesty. We always have and always will.*"

*Damon*

*Damon and Quincy Jones*

*me, Mark and Alan, they gave me a wonderful birthday party*

Jerry and Ilene Sraberg

Hal David, me and Eunice David

## Anyone Who Had A Heart

Mary Ann Simone,
John Simone and Eunice Peterson

*"Waiter, we'd like to eat.", Philip Michael Thomas and me*

# My Point

# Of View

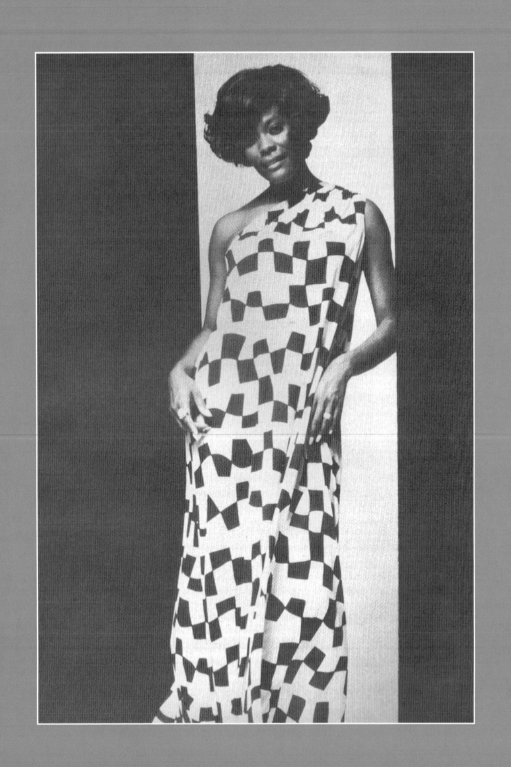

Dionne Warwick has, over an illustrious four-decade career, established herself as an international musical legend. Her reputation as a hit maker has been firmly etched into public consciousness, thanks to nearly sixty charted hits since "Don't Make Me Over" began its climb up the charts in December 1962. As a performer, she has charmed and entertained audiences on every continent, amassing a worldwide audience. There are a few important "firsts" that make Dionne Warwick a true pioneer.

Dionne Warwick received her first Grammy Award in 1968 (for the classic "Do You Know The Way to San Jose?"), and in so doing became the first African-American solo female artist of her generation to win the prestigious award for Best Contemporary Female Vocal Performance. This award has only been awarded to one other female African-American legend, Ella Fitzgerald. Other African-American female recording artists certainly racked up their share of crossover pop and R&B hits during the 1960's. However, Dionne Warwick preceded the mainstream success of some of her musical peers by becoming the first such artist to rack up a dozen consecutive Top 100 hit singles from 1963 to 1966.

Dionne Warwick's performance at the Olympia Theater in Paris (1963) rocketed her to international stardom. As she was establishing herself as a major force in American contemporary music, she steadily gained in popularity among European audiences. Hits like

*I Love Paris*

"Anyone Who Had A Heart" and "Walk On By" brought successively larger visibility and success around the world. In 1968 she became the first African-American female performer to appear before the Queen of England at a Royal Command Performance. Since then, Dionne has performed before numerous kings, queens, presidents, and heads of state. Her recordings of songs like "A House Is Not A home," "Alfie," "(Theme From) The Valley Of The Dolls," and "The April Fools" made Dionne Warwick a pioneer as one of the first female artists to popularize classic movie themes. In 1968 Dionne made her own film debut in the movie "Slaves". This marked the first time, since Lena Horne, that a contemporary African-American female recording artist achieved such a goal.

In recent years, Dionne's pioneering efforts have focused on leading the music industry in the fight against AIDS. Her Grammy-winning, chart topping, single "That's What Friends Are For," lead the way by raising, literally, millions of dollars for AIDS research.

*Throughout the world, Dionne has devoted countless hours to a wide range of humanitarian causes, serving as the US-Ambassador for Health throughout the Eighties. On October 16, 2002 she was named a global Ambassador for the United Nations' Food and Agriculture Organization (FAO), based in Rome, Italy. Dionne has spearheaded the long overdue development and production of a history book that will detail African and African-American history for use in schools, libraries, and bookstores throughout the world. She continues her work as a socially conscious and concerned global citizen.*

*With a legacy of accomplishments and achievements, Dionne Warwick is proudly celebrating her 40th year in the recording industry. She is planning a new 2003 release CD composed of duets with her peers entitled "My Friends And Me". Dionne says, "This is one of the most exciting recording projects for me and I am looking forward to getting it out as soon as possible for everyone to enjoy." This new album can trace its roots to the very earliest years of her amazing musical career. Dionne began singing during her childhood years in East Orange, New Jersey, initially in church. Occasionally she sang as a soloist and fill-in voice for the renowned "Drinkard Singers", a group comprised of her mother Lee along with her aunts and uncles. During her teens, Dionne and sister Dee Dee started their own gospel group, "The Gospelaires". It was while visiting the Drinkard Singers at the famed Apollo Theater in Harlem that Dionne was asked to sing backup during a session for saxophonist Sam "The Man" Taylor. In February 1998, the Apollo Theater paid tribute to Dionne in a spe-cial event highlighting her constant support for the venue and her work as a music trailblazer. While attending The Hartt College Of Music in Hartford, Connecticut, she began making trips to do regular session work in New York. She sang behind many of the biggest starts of the 1960's including Dinah Washington, Brook Benton, Chuck Jackson, and Solomon Burke to name a few. Once Burt Bacharach, composer, arranger, and producer heard her singing during a session for The Drifters, he asked her to sing on demos of songs he was writing with new partner Hal David. In 1962, Bacharach & David presented one such demo to Scepter Records. The label President, Florence Greenberg, did not want the song; she did, however, want the voice and Dionne began a hit-filled, twelve-year, association with the New York label. In all, Dionne, Burt, and Hal racked up thirty hit singles, and close to twenty best-selling albums, during their first decade together. Songs like "Do You Know The Way To San Jose," "Message To Michael," "This Girl's In Love With You," "I'll Never Fall In Love Again," and "Reach Out For Me," established Dionne Warwick as a consummate artist and performer. Known as the artist who "bridged the gap," Dionne's soulful blend of pop, gospel and R&B music transcended race, culture, and musical boundaries.*

## My Point Of View

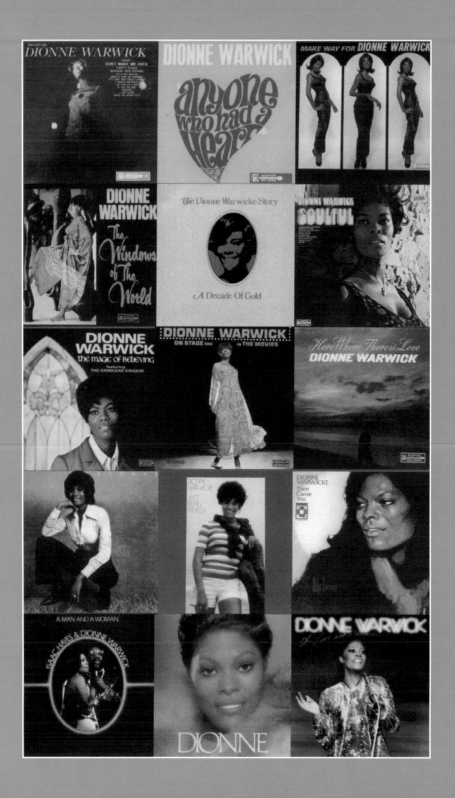

In 1970, Dionne received her second Grammy Award for the best-selling album "I'll Never Fall In Love Again" and she began her second decade of hits by signing with Warner Brothers Records. Dionne recorded half-a-dozen albums, working with top producers like Thom Bell, Holland-Dozier-Holland, Jerry Ragavoy, Steve Barri, and Michael Omartian. In 1974 she hit the top of the charts for the first time with "Then Came You," a million-selling duet with The Spinners. Three years later, she teamed up with Isaac Hayes for a highly successful world tour, "A Man And A Woman."

In 1976, fresh from earning a Master's Degree in Music from her alma mater (The Hartt College of Music), Dionne signed with Arista Records, beginning a third decade of hit-making. Label-mate Barry Manilow produced her first Platinum-selling album "Dionne". The album included these back-to-back hits; "I'll Never Love This Way Again," and "Déjà Vu." Both recordings earned Grammy Awards, making Dionne the first female artist to win the Best Female Pop, and Best Female R&B Performance, Award. Hot on the heels of her phenomenal success, Dionne began her first stint as host for the highly successful television show "Solid Gold". Further milestones marked Dionne's tenure with Arista. Her 1982 album, Heartbreaker, co-produced by Barry Gibb and The Bee Gees, became an international chart-topper. In 1985, Dionne reunited with producer Burt Bacharach, and longtime friends Gladys Knight, Stevie Wonder, and Elton John to record the classic "That's What Friends Are For." Profits from the sale of that song were donated to the American Foundation for AIDS Research (AmFAR). In 1990 she joined forces with a number of Arista label-mates to raise over $2.5 Million for various AIDS organizations during the star-studded "That's What Friends Are For" Benefit at New York's Radio City Music Hall. Dionne's album "Friends" achieved Gold status. Throughout the Eighties she collaborated with many of her musical peers, including Johnny Mathis, Smokey Robinson, Luther Vandross and others. Dionne worked with Stevie Wonder as music coordinator for the film and Academy Award winning soundtrack album The Woman In Red. She was one of the key participants in the all-star charity single "We Are The World" and, in 1984 she performed at "Live Aid". In addition to co-hosting and helping to launch "The Soul Train Music Awards", she also starred in her own show, "Dionne And Friends." She was co-executive producer of "Celebrate The Soul Of American Music" which honored and recognized many of her fellow musical pioneers. Throughout the 1980's and 1990's, Dionne toured extensively with Burt Bacharach.

*Enjoy Every Day*

*The show won rave reviews from fans and press alike for reinforcing the timeless musical legacy of the Bacharach, David and Warwick team. Her recent musical achievements have included performances as part of the "National Symphony With The Divas," and, in Tokyo, performances with The National Opera Company of Japan; yes, Dionne even signs classical music. Her recent activities have included the creation of Carr / Todd / Warwick Production, Inc. The goal of the organization is to produce television and film projects. For the past fifteen years she has worked tirelessly as the co-founder of the Dionne Warwick Design Group, Inc. With partner Bruce Garrick, Dionne has been responsible for designing numerous international projects ranging from private estates to world-class hotels which, she notes, are "all affordable!" In 2002 Dionne was featured on a Home & Garden Network show highlighting the Palm Desert home designed by her and her partner Bruce. Dionne now divides her time equally between Brazil and the United States, and has made the design of her Brazilian home a special project. In 1994, Dionne's final album for Arista was the critically acclaimed "Aquarela Do Brasil" (Watercolor of Brazil) that showcased her long-term love affair with the people and music of Brazil.*

*Dionne's status as a musical icon and humanitarian is legendary. With her own star on the Hollywood Walk of Fame, she continues to work tirelessly with various organizations dedicated to empowering and inspiring others. In 1997 she was awarded the "Luminary Award" by the American Society of Young Musicians. That same year she*

### Friends

*joined General Colin Powell in celebrating the tenth anniversary of the "Best Friends" Program, an abstinence and character-building program for young women. Dionne's East Orange New Jersey Elementary School, Lincoln Elementary, honored her by renaming it "The Dionne Warwick Institute of Economics and Entrepreneurship." Displaying her own business skills, Dionne plans to reactivate her skin care regimen and fragrance in 2003. In early 1998, the National Association of Record Merchandisers (NARM) gave Dionne the Chairman's Award for Sustained Creative Achievement. In November 2001, the History Makers Organization of Chicago named her "History Maker". 2002 was a special year for Dionne; she was honored by the American Red Ribbon AIDS Foundation; in October she was named FAO Ambassador of the United Nations; in December she was honored by The Recording Academy with the 2002 New York Chapter's Heroes Award and she appeared (for the fourth time) on the Vatican's Christmas Concert. In 2003, she received a lifetime achievement award from the R&B Foundation, and she was selected as one of the "2003 Top Faces of Black History".*

# Credits

# Credits

Bill Jones

Clarence Waldren

David Vance

Harry Langdon

Naras

The Many Fans, Family

Friends Who Contributed Personal Photos

# Impressum

"My Point Of View", Dionne Warwick

First Edition 2003

© by Mastropaolo & Koblischek Editor,
Lindau im Bodensee 2003

Design: Giorgio Paolo Mastropaolo

Credits: Dionne Warwick, Ingo Koblischek,
Context GmbH, Henry Carr, Carlos Keyes,
Christa Becker-Obi, families and friends

Printed by Memminger MedienCentrum AG

www.mastropaolokoblischek.com

„I remember the time my brother, and my of ice cream in Las Vegas from wasn't too thrilled. David got a good I mean). We were young and for this one exception."

cousin Barry ordered 1.100 US$ worth

room service. Boy, when mom found out she

old fashioned  talking to (if you know what

the record pretty good kids with

Damon

*... and now, finally,*

*... enjoy the music!*